G000269029

A BOOT UP

ULLSWATER

Keith Wood

First published in Great Britain in 2009

British Library Cataloguing-in-Publication Data
A CIP record for this title is available from the British Library

ISBN 978 1 906887 12 4

PiXZ Books
Halsgrove House, Ryelands Industrial Estate,
Bagley Road, Wellington, Somerset TA21 9PZ
Tel: 01823 653777
Fax: 01823 216796
email: sales@halsgrove.com

An imprint of Halstar Ltd, part of the Halsgrove group of companies
Information on all Halsgrove titles is available at: www.halsgrove.com

Printed and bound by Grafiche Flaminia, Italy

Contents

How to use this book

Ullswater, the most north-easterly of the lakes, offers great walking opportunities for either the experienced fell-walker or those seeking a more gentle stroll at lower level amongst its spectacular and varied scenery. Although the key tourist spots of Pooley Bridge and Glenridding can be busy at peaks times, quiet footpaths and bridleways are quickly reached and the tranquillity of the area can be truly appreciated.

At nine miles long, Ullswater is the second largest lake in the Lake District. It is a typical narrow ribbon lake formed, with its close neighbour Brothers Water, when the glaciers retreated at the end of the last ice age. The surrounding mountains, including the Helvellyn range, give Ullswater its shape as it zigzags across the landscape.

Whatever the time of year, the views are breathtaking; from Wordsworth's famous daffodils at the water's edge heralding the spring, through the nodding bluebells of May to the magnificent russets and golds of autumn leaves and the ice-blue snow-capped peaks of winter, they never fail to impress.

Accessible from the M6 Motorway at Junction 40, the nearby market town of Penrith is also on the West Coast Main Rail Line. Information about public transport to Pooley Bridge, Glenridding and Patterdale from Penrith Station is provided by Traveline; the services are fairly frequent. The start points for several of the walks are from the main centres or on public transport routes (Walks 2, 7,8,9), the others will need private cars.

One of Ullswater's attractions is the Ullswater 'Steamers' which provide trips around the lake calling at Pooley Bridge, Glenridding and Howtown (Walk 2 makes use of the service from Pooley Bridge to Howtown). Details are available from Ullswater Steamers, The Pier House, Glenridding 017684 82229; www.ullswater-steamers.co.uk.

- The majority of walks in this book are relatively easy to moderate and offer pleasant walking in this beautiful and varied landscape. For the more adventurous Beda Fell, Sheffield Pike, Red Tarn (walks 5, 8 and 9) give a taste of true, mountain walking.

- Each route is graded from Easy to More Challenging with further details of distance, height ascended and the type of terrain covered, to help with decisions of which walk to choose. The majority of the walks have details of refreshments and facilities available – usually at the end, however, for some this requires a minor detour or short car journey.

- All ten walks are covered by the Ordnance Survey Explorer Map OL5: The English Lakes, North-Eastern area, and Harvey's Lakeland East and Lakeland Central Maps. The maps in this book are only an outline version of each walk and the detail provided by the OS maps puts each route in context.

- Every year tens of thousands of visitors enjoy the fells with the vast majority coming to no harm. However there are many cases each year where walkers are injured, get lost or find themselves in some other kind of difficulty requiring the assistance of the Mountain Rescue Services. A few simple precautions should help avoid any problems:

- If you are unsure about your fitness start with the walks graded Easy and work your way up to More Challenging.

- Wear suitable footwear- properly fitted walking boots are recommended for all the walks.

- Take suitable clothing; the weather in the Lake District can change very quickly, take a waterproof and extra warm layers to wear.

- Take plenty to eat and drink en route, dehydration and lack of nourishment can lead to fatigue and mistakes being made. An outline map illustrates each walk but it is recommended that a complete map is taken.

- Inform someone of your planned route and expected return time. Check the weather forecast in advance and only take to the more challenging routes on clear days.

- And finally keep to the paths and watch where you are putting your feet – most accidents are caused by careless slips!

Useful websites:

Lake District National Park
www.lake-district.gov.uk
National Trust
www.nationaltrust.org.uk
Friends of the Lake District
www.fld.org.uk
Cumbria Tourist Board
www.cumbria-the-lake-district.co.uk
Cumbria Tourism
www.golakes.co.uk
Lake District Outdoors
www.lakedistrictoutdoors.co.uk.
Dalemain
www.dalemain.co.uk.
Ullswater Steamers Ltd
www.ullswater-steamers.co.uk.
Traveline – Public Transport Information
www.traveline.org.uk
Keith Wood Photography
www.keithwoodphotography.co.uk

Key to Symbols Used

Level of difficulty:

Easy 🤍

Fair 🤍 🤍

More challenging 🤍 🤍 🤍

Map symbols:

🚗 Park & start

―――― Tarred Road

----- Footpath

■ Building

♥ Pub

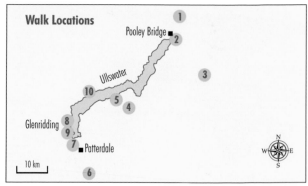

Walk Locations

1 Dacre & Dalemain

Enjoy a full length view of the lake and Borrowdale from this popular viewpoint

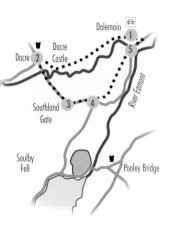

Level: 🥾
Length: 3½ miles (5.5km)
Ascent: 300 feet (100m)
Terrain: Easy walking on farm and country lanes with a return on a field path.
Park & start: Dalemain (GR 477 270).
Info: Check the Dalemain website for opening times (normally closed Friday and Saturday). www.dalemain.com.
Refreshments & facilities: Dalemain Mediaeval Hall Tearoom. Fox and Hounds, Dacre.

Dalemain, one of the finest historic houses in North Lakeland, makes an ideal start for this short walk just north of Ullswater. The house itself is unashamedly an English gentleman's country residence without the pretensions of a stately home. Early records show that a fortified pele tower was built on the Dalemain site during the reign of Henry II to guard against marauding Border Reivers. Home to the Hasell family since 1679 the house has a friendly and homely feel and the tranquility of the well-maintained gardens are in stark contrast to the honey pot of nearby Pooley Bridge. The walk up to Dacre passing by Dacre Castle coupled with a visit to Dalemain and its gardens makes for a great day out for all ages.

1000 m

Starting from the Dalemain Estate Car Park to the side of the main house, walk through the outbuildings around the back of the house following the yellow waymarker sign into the courtyard. Pass under an arch between the buildings and into the impressive stable yard. Bear around to the right over the cobbles onto the lane between two walls. This lane with woods on either side heads up to the small village of **Dacre** with Dacre Beck below on the left. Pass through a gate into the next large field, keeping to the right-hand field boundary, and enjoy this easy walking

Dalemain

Little is known about the curious carved-stone Dacre Bears. They are said to tell the story of a sleeping bear which is jumped on by a cat or lynx; the bear tries to dislodge the cat; finally, having eaten the cat it sits looking extremely satisfied!

on the level. Through another gate, the track swings around to the right up towards the village. As the track swings around rising gently, pass by several farm buildings and then the impressive **Dacre Castle**, a fourteenth-century sandstone walled pele tower, part of the Dalemain estate since being bought by Edward Hasell in 1723.

Dacre Bear

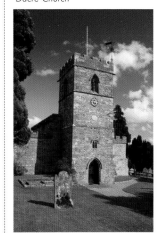

Dacre Church

(2) As the track emerges onto the road in the middle of **Dacre** village, take a detour to visit the churchyard, following the path immediately to the right in front of a barn across the adjacent pasture. The ancient picturesque parish of Dacre has had a church on this site for over a thousand years. In the church parts of two ancient crosses survive, one of which pre-dates the Vikings. It is said that they illustrate Adam and Eve and the sacrifice of Isaac. Having explored the churchyard and visited the Dacre Bears , return to the road. Turn left and head down this quiet road through the village and down to the valley bottom and Dacre Beck. The road crossing the beck swings around to the left passing a picnic area and continues heading up the hill towards **Souland Gate**. Pass by the Old Vicarage, an impressive house on the left and continue on this quiet lane over the brow of the hill.

Dacre Castle

(3) The road passes by Soulands Gate farm buildings on the left. Whilst this is a quiet road be alert to any traffic and keep to the right hand side of the road. As the road starts to descend there is a fine view across to **Arthurs Pike** and **Bonscale Pike**.

(4) The road reaches the busy A592 Penrith to Pooley Bridge road and at the junction a Pubic Footpath sign leads to a path through a red sandstone stile. Over the stile, follow the path across the field cutting the corner and cross the wooden stile into the next field. Follow the vague path through this next field keeping to the left hand field boundary. The green farmer's track rises to the top of the field. At the end of the field go over the next wooden stile, keep to the track running along the edge of the field. Cross the stile into the next field and keep heading along with the wood on the left hand side. Beyond the next field, **Dalemain** comes into view. Over another stile, a clearer track cuts diagonally across this last field heading towards the road.

(5) As there is no access across the front of the house, a short walk along the road is necessary here. Avoiding the obvious farm gate, head to the far corner of the field to cross over a wooden stile next to an iron gate and onto the road. Turn left, crossing over the ornamental bridge over Dacre Beck and walk next to the road for a hundred yards in front of the house. All that remains is to head back up the drive to return to the Estate Car Park.

Post box in Dacre

Dalemain

2 **Ullswater's Eastern Shoreline**

Combine a cruise on the lake with a return walking on the Eastern shoreline

Level:
Length: 5¹/₃ miles (8.5km)
Ascent: 600 feet (180m)
Terrain: Level walking most of the way with a gentle pull up to the Cock Pit with a steady descent back to Pooley Bridge.
Park & start: LDNP Car Park in Pooley Bridge (GR 471 243).
Info: Ullswater Steamer times from www.ullswater-steamers.co.uk
Refreshments & facilities: Public houses and Tearooms, Pooley Bridge; Howtown Hotel.

No visit to the Ullswater area would be complete without a trip on the lake. The Ullswater 'Steamers' have been sailing on this most beautiful of England's lakes for almost one hundred and fifty years and are the perfect way to enjoy the area. The 'Steamer' routes provide the perfect opportunity to link together the many paths and bridleways of the area, giving access to the more remote eastern shoreline. For most walkers, linear routes are often not possible due to the problems of arranging for dropping off and picking up at the finish. However this delightful route, the only linear walk in the book, takes advantage of the regular service of the Ullswater Steamers, to arrive at the start.

1 Park in one of the LDNP Car parks in **Pooley Bridge**, walk to the Ullswater Steamer Landing stage and take the boat to the **Howtown Landings**. From the boat the impressive ridge of **Arthur's Pike** and **Bonscale Pike** along the left shore of the lake can be seen.

Ullswater Steamer

Pooley Bridge Landings

Leave the steamer at the Howtown Landings and from the landing stage walk to the Pooley Bridge to Howtown road, turning right onto the road heading towards the hamlet of **Howtown**. Walk along the quiet lane with Hallin Fell on the right and approach Howtown on the left. At the minor junction with the Howtown Hotel sign opposite a Victorian Post Box, turn left and head into the hamlet itself. Walk along the lane past the Howtown Hotel on the right and continue through the back of the village keeping to the lane.

2 As the road forks head left through the trees up to

Mellguards. Walk through the yard and at the end of the lane pass through a wooden gate to emerge onto a clear path above the wall. Head left along this clear path above the houses passing by a copse of trees on the right enclosed by a drystone wall. Continue on the path where there is a fine view just down to the left to the landings and Hallin Fell behind. As the path makes its way along with a drystone wall just below to the left, the Bay of Howtown Wyke is left behind. Here there are spectacular views across the lake to the boathouses on the far side with Gowbarrow Fell above. Walking beneath the heights of Bonscale Pike and looking carefully

Steamer at Howtown Landings

above on the skyline, the rectangular shape of Bonscale Tower can be seen above the crags.

3   Approaching **Swarth Beck** and a copse of trees, ignore the gate with a blue marker heading to the left. Keep to the main path with the wall still on the left signed Public Bridleway Pooley Bridge. Around the copse of trees, cross over the tumbling Swarth Beck and keep to the clear

Howtown Hotel

Hallin Fell from shoreline path

Auterstone Wood. The path keeps gently rising, slowly gaining height above the lake. The path starts to level off as it passes the wood of **Barton Park** on the left with fellside opening out to the front right. The path continues rising gently above Barton Park.

(4) Reaching the edge of the enclosure of Barton Park at **Aik Beck** there is a clear Bridleway Sign. Cross the beck and follow the main path straight ahead. The path now crosses **Moor Divock** up above Pooley Bridge. (There are further

stony path, the crags of Arthur's Pike towering above. Pass by the edge of a boulder field, strewn with rocks which have crashed down from the crags of Arthur's Pike above. Where an indistinct green path forks off to the left to follow the wall, keep to the main track heading upwards along the base of Arthur's Pike. Just above the path there is a well built stone tower in the middle of nowhere next to

Ullswater from shoreline path

The Cockpit

the moor. Keep to the well made path across the marshy section of the moor.

(6) At a large pile of stones marking a cross roads of paths with the main bridleway across the moor, turn left to head down the wide unsurfaced track down towards Pooley Bridge with fantastic panoramic views along Ullswater. The outline of **Blencathra** can be seen perfectly

The River Eamont flows out of Ullswater at Pooley Bridge. The village takes its name from a large pool in the river just before the outflow and the spanning of the river by a bridge in the 16th century. The pool no longer exists but a bridge still crosses the river.

opportunities to explore more of Moor Divock in the next walk in this book.) Keep to the most well worn of all the paths straight on across this moorland and eventually the Neolithic stone circle known as **the Cockpit** can be seen on a green island of

short cropped grass.

(5) Arriving at the Cockpit, spend a while to walk around this mysterious and ancient site. Pass by the Cockpit and take the left hand of the two main tracks heading across

against the sky, giving rise to its other name of Saddleback. Continue walking downhill on a great track straight down to Pooley Bridge, heading initially down to Roehead.

Pass through the gate which marks the edge of the moor and onto the road, past the houses at Roehead and down the road towards Pooley Bridge.

7 At the crossroads at the bottom of the lane go straight across to go into Pooley Bridge walking along the pavement back to the start point.

Dunmallard and Pooley Bridge

3 **Moor Divock**

An enticing walk with the ancients, rewarded by a spectacular Ullswater vista

Moor Divock is an antiquarian's delight. There is ample evidence that some of Lakeland's earliest inhabitants chose to live here. Many walkers will be familiar with the Roman road of "High Street" from Ambleside to Brougham and indeed part of this walk follows its route, but this gentle stroll across Moor Divock gives chance to study the remains of a much earlier civilisation. Three sites are visited on the route, starting with the "Cop Stone" now a lonely monolith, the sole survivor of a stone circle. The second point of interest is a

Level:
Length: 4½ miles (7km)
Ascent: 400 feet (125m)
Terrain: Good clear paths across open moorland.
Park and start: Roadside 1 mile above Helton (Grid ref 497 214).
Refreshments & facilities: Queens Head; Punch Bowl, Askham.

nearby small circle of stones, giving away its true identity as a collapsed burial mound, where a food vessel and human remains were found when it was excavated. The final antiquity is the "Cockpit", a complete and impressive Neolithic stone circle dating back over 4000 years.

19

In addition to the historic features, it's worth saving this one for a clear day because there are exceptional full-length views down Ullswater from Heughscar Hill, the highest point of the walk.

(1) There is ample space to park the car at the roadside at the start of the walk on the minor road crossing the moor out of the back of the village of **Helton**. Leave the car by the short Public Bridleway Sign Roe Head 2m, Widewath ½m. Set off along the wide bridleway heading towards **Roe Head** with **the Cop Stone** already in sight from the road. Follow the track, taking a minor 10 yard detour to inspect the Cop Stone with fine views looking across the moor to Loadpot and Wether Hill.

The Cop Stone

Resume the walk along the wide velvet green bridleway, which predates the arrival of the Romans. The summit of **Heughscar Hill**, the high point of the walk, and a copse of trees can be seen to the front right. The collapsed burial mound can be found about ⅓ mile from the Cop Stone. Its exact location is a few yards to the right of

the bridleway through the bracken and a minor track can usually be seen leading to it. Return to the main bridleway to continue the journey across the moor.

(2) Take the first clear track off to the right through the bracken, heading towards the gap between the

Collapsed burial mound

Heather on Moor Divock

two stands of trees on the horizon. This track offers fine walking across the moor between the bracken and heather with views towards the Eden Valley and across to the Pennines on the right where Cross Fell and the radar station can be seen on a clear day. The track passes by a series of old industrial spoil heaps. Shortly after passing the spoil heaps the track splits, take the left hand fork gently rising towards Heughscar Hill.

3 At the brow of the hill between the two stands of trees join the main bridleway up from Askham, turning left to complete the gentle climb, past the trees to reach the summit of Heughscar Hill, marked by a small pile of stones. The summit offers fantastic views looking along Ullswater, with the whole of the walk laid out below, including **the Cockpit**. Continue the journey along the edge of the hill initially on the bridleway

and then as the bridleway veers away to the right keep to the edge of the scar to reach the clear limestone outcrop of Heughscar from whence the hill gets its name.

4 From the top of the scar a narrow path heads down through the bracken to join a worn bridleway coming from the right and heading towards **Arthur's Pike** on the left. Turn left onto this bridleway and follow the clear track, ignoring other paths to the left and right. The route now follows in the footsteps of the Romans along High Street with outstanding views along the length of Ullswater to Hallin Fell and Place Fell with Hellvellyn on the horizon. As the track starts to gently lose height a stone circle appears directly

During Neolithic times the population of Cumbria increased as people moved inland from the coastal areas. Stone circles and henges began to be constructed; these included the impressive henge at Mayburgh near Penrith and its close neighbour King Arthur's Round Table, as well as the famous Castlerigg Stone Circle near Keswick.

in front, this is the Cockpit – the next destination.

5 Where **High Street** crosses the main bridleway across the moor continue straight across heading along the dry path to the Cockpit. Up

until recently this path was a horrible marshy bog to cross, described by Wainwright in his guide to 'The Far Eastern Fells' as "positively the worst bog on any regular Lakeland path".

6 The Cockpit is a remarkably complete stone circle, dating back 4,000 years to the Neolithic period. The purpose of such sites can only be surmised but must have been

important to the ancient people who lived here. From the circle take the other clear path back across the marsh towards the main bridleway.

7 Upon reaching the main bridleway at **Ketley Gate**, turn right to follow the track as it heads back across the moor, eventually rejoining the outward route and returning to the start and your car.

The Cockpit

Ketley Gate

Rock art on Moor Divock

Bracken fronds

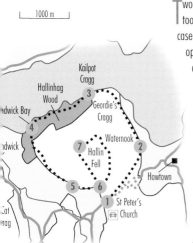

4 **Hallin Fell**

A circuit around a little fell with delightful lake and mountain views

Two for the price of one, sounds too good to be true, but not in the case of Hallin Fell which offers the opportunity to enjoy separately or to combine two short and delightful walks ideally suited to a half day. At barely 1000ft, Hallin Fell stands proud surrounded by higher fells midway along Ullswater's eastern shore. Set at the head of two of Lakeland's most tranquil and beautiful valleys, Boredale and Martindale, the walk offers full length views down both. The start point for

Level: 🥾 🥾
Length: 3 miles (4½ km) and 1 mile (1½ km)
Ascent: 750 feet total (225m)
Terrain: Generally easy walking, with a steep climb through woodland leaving the lake shore.
Park and start: Opposite St Peter's Church above Howtown (Grid ref 435 192).
Refreshments & facilities: Howtown Hotel.

the walk, high above the pretty hamlet of Howtown, can be reached by the narrow road from Pooley Bridge along Ullswater's east bank passing the famous Sharrow Bay Country House Hotel.

1 Park opposite the "new" church of St Peter, Martindale. The walk starts by heading down along the road towards **Howtown** for about 200 yards, passing the estate sign for Dalemain, Martindale, Hallin Fell and The Hause. At a gravel and salt pile, a distinctive track turns left away from the road heading towards Ullswater. Walking down the track dramatic views unfold along Ullswater looking towards Pooley Bridge and Dunmallard Hill at the head of the lake. The path passes an old iron bench of the Lake District Association and continuing on drops down towards the lake with the Howtown landings coming into view together with the cairn on **Arthur's Pike** on the skyline to the front right.

2 As the path starts to swing round to the left another track joins from the right bringing the intake wall to your right. The path now becomes a little rougher and regains some height, before continuing along with the intake wall always on the right. This part of the walk now follows along the Howtown to Patterdale path, with fine views across Ullswater. After passing a few oak trees, the path leaves the wall and swings round to the left again around **Geordie's Crag** with Gowbarrow Fell coming into view on the opposite side of the lake. The path now passes

Arthur's Pike from Geordie's Crag

Martindale Old Church

years have adorned the smooth beech bark on many of the trees. Locals and visitors alike have written messages, proclamations of love or simply recorded their presence. Many dates throughout the last century are recorded as far back as 1903, however 1066 might not have been original!! The beech trees soon give way to oak

through some oak trees before opening out again at the shoreline and coming to a wall.

3 Pass through the kissing gate in the wall to enter **Hallinhag Wood**. This first part of the wood contains a mass of mature beech trees and a tangle of exposed roots. Take the opportunity to inspect the numerous carvings with which people over the

The 16th century church of St Martin, nestling in Martindale is a worthwhile extra. On this site since at least the thirteenth century, inside there is a font which may have started life as a Roman altar. The yew tree in the churchyard predates all this, being about 1300 years old.

woodland with its characteristic rough bark and so the carvings cease. The path undulates between the trees along the lakeshore.

4 Approaching **Sandwick Bay**, a wall appears in front, with another gate. Just before the gate, take a faint track veering off up through the wood to the left leaving

Looking across Ullswater from Kailpot Crag

the main shoreline path. This narrow track goes steeply uphill through the oak wood, with the wall to the right all the way up. At the top corner of the wood pass through a kissing gate back onto the open fellside above the intake wall to the right. The summit crags of **Hallin Fell** come into view to the left. The path continues to steadily rise along the fellside and swings around again. A panoramic view opens out with Beda Fell dominating the middle ground, Place Fell to the right and the quiet valley

Scots pines on Kailpot Crag

Hallin Fell summit cairn

of Boredale between the two with Boredale Hause at its end. The path passes a broken down barn with views down to **Sandwick Beck**.

5 Just after passing a lonely Scots pine, the path crosses another track and continues straight

on; the full beauty of Martindale with the deer sanctuary of the Nab dominating the end of the valley. Continue walking along parallel with the intake wall until the wall turns to head down the fellside.

Howtown from Hallin Fell

Martindale from Hallin Fell

6 It's decision time. Either turn right and simply follow the broad track of smooth short cropped grass back down to the start
Or
Take the left track up the fell. The path shortly splits into 3 branches, take the middle one directly to the superb 12ft high summit cairn and enjoy the panoramic views of Ullswater.

7 From the summit, rather than simply reversing the ascent, head north east losing some height before swinging sharply round to the south along a clear track which leads back to intake wall and back to the car.

Place Fell from Hallin Fell

5 Beda Fell & Ullswater

Enjoy a walk in two halves above tranquil, unspoilt valleys, returning along busier lakeside paths

Level: 🥾 🥾 🥾
Length: 8 miles (13km)
Ascent: 2100 feet (640m)
Terrain: Steady ascent up Beda Fell, returning by a clear and popular shoreline path.
Park and start: Sandwick Village (Grid ref NY423 196).
Refreshments & facilities: Patterdale Hotel (short detour required).

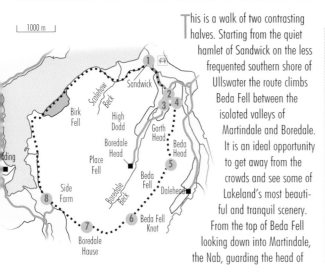

This is a walk of two contrasting halves. Starting from the quiet hamlet of Sandwick on the less frequented southern shore of Ullswater the route climbs Beda Fell between the isolated valleys of Martindale and Boredale. It is an ideal opportunity to get away from the crowds and see some of Lakeland's most beautiful and tranquil scenery. From the top of Beda Fell looking down into Martindale, the Nab, guarding the head of

the dale can be seen. From this quiet back-water the route changes character as it then follows the popular path next to Ullswater around the base of Place Fell back to Sandwick.

1 In the hamlet of **Sandwick** there is space for about nine or ten cars on the grass at the end of the road. Park here and start walking back along the road towards **Martindale**. Continue to walk down this beautiful, tranquil lane surrounded by open fellside to the right and mixed woodland beside the beck on the left. **Hallin Fell** is immediately to the left, **Beda Fell** is straight ahead and **Place Fell** to the right.

Mist over Ullswater and Gowbarrow Fell from the ridge

Beda Fell across Ullswater

2 Reaching the road with its traditional striped and crested signpost, turn right following the 'Patterdale Footpath only' sign heading along the road towards **Garth Head Farm**.

3 At **Garth Head** the road continues to the remote farms of upper **Boredale**, footpaths going to both left and right. Directly after the barn on the left of the road notice the sign in the wall next to the black house gate to 'Martindale', climb over the fence via a stile and head straight up the fellside between two stone walls. The walls open out and the green path continues quite steeply up the fellside to reach the ridgeline. After a short climb an iron seat is

These valleys and fells are a sanctuary for red deer which can be seen clearly during the summer months, their red coats standing out against the lush grass and bracken. Often to be heard during the autumn rutting season, they are more difficult to spot as the foliage changes to a deep russet providing perfect camouflage.

reached on the ridge with views down into **Martindale** and back towards Howtown.

4 Turn right onto the ridge following the path as it winds its way through rocky outcrops gradually gaining height. To the left the full length of Martindale comes into view with the red roofs of The Bungalow, a former hunting lodge of the Dalemain Estate at the head of the valley and to the right the isolated farm buildings in upper Boredale. There is a short stretch on the level before the final climb. As the path starts to rise on the final stretch to the top the path forks, both arrive at the summit but the preferred route is the right hand path going straight up the rocks in front.

5 After a short but steep climb, the path levels out and winds its way to the first cairn on **Beda Head**. Looking behind, the vast expanse of Ullswater can be seen

Hallin Fell from the Beda Fell ridge

heading towards Pooley Bridge, and beyond views to Penrith and the Pennines on the horizon. On reaching the first cairn there is a small stone shelter on the Boredale side. Walk on to the second cairn; the true summit and highest point on the walk at 1676 feet. The summit provides a panoramic view. From here head across the broad spongy path keeping St Sunday Crag directly to the front - this area can be boggy in wet weather. After meandering gently for a while the path rises steeply again approaching **Beda Fell Knott**.

6 A short walk takes you to a crossroads of paths; from the left the path comes up from Martindale, straight on the path goes to **Angle Tarn** - take the path to the right to

Beda Fell summit

Boredale Hause, swinging down and round, before crossing over Freeze Beck.

(7) Make your way across Boredale Hause using one of the myriad of paths before picking up the main path down towards

Sheffield Pike from Boredale Hause

Patterdale. Walk across a flat grassy area past former mine-workings. The path splits, heading down to Brothers Water on the left, take the route down to the right heads towards Patterdale and **Glenridding**. After a short distance the path forks again, take the left fork heading straight down towards the trees behind the houses in Patterdale.

(8) On reaching the cottages at Patterdale follow the path down in front of Place Fell Cottage and through a gate onto a road. Once through the gate immediately turn right through another gate following the signpost 'Public Bridleway'. Continue on the Bridleway behind Side Farm End and **Side Farm**. Look for a slate sign on the wall to

Martindale deer

Howtown and **Sandwick**; the route now following the well-worn and popular route back to Sandwick. There are extensive views across the lake as the path follows the shoreline. The path undulates through woodland with several steep climbs along the way. Upon reaching **Scalehow Force** the beck is crossed by a wooden bridge and the path continues on to eventually return to Sandwick at the end of a great walk.

Sheffield Pike and Place Fell from Boredale Hause

6 Brothers Water & Hartsop

Enjoy a stroll through a Conservation Area with lilied lake and ancient hamlet

| 1000 m |

This is a popular low level walk, equally suited to a wet winter's day, crisp frosty morning or, a sunny summer's evening. Looking down on Brothers Water from Kirkstone Pass it is easy to imagine how Brothers Water was probably an extension of Ullswater at the end of the last ice age. It eventually became a separate lake in its own right as silt and debris washed down from the surrounding fells over the intervening millennia. The walk follows the lakeshore before passing through the picturesque hamlet of Hartsop. Now quiet, Hartsop was formally a hive of industrial activity

Level: 🥾

Length: 4 ½ miles (7km)

Ascent: 250ft in total (75m)

Terrain: Good paths throughout, couple of stiles to go over.

Park and start: Cow Bridge LDNP Car Park (Grid ref 403134)

Refreshments & facilities: Brotherswater Inn.

with two mines and quarries above on Caudale Moor; the population was once bigger than that of Patterdale or Glenridding. The buildings are from the 17th century and have characteristic stepped gables, circular chimneys and 'spinning galleries'.

Brothers Water

1 Park in Cow Bridge Car Park to the north of Brothers Water near the village of **Hartsop**. Leave the car park through a gate onto a well made track. The walk beside **Goldrill Beck** heading towards Brother's Water passes through the hazel and oak of **Low Wood**. Upon reaching the lakeshore the path continues on rising slightly before returning to the level of the lake, looking across the lake to the shapely dome of Hartsop Dodd, with Grey Crag on the horizon. The track continues through the end of the woods and quickly reaches the head of the lake before continuing on to **Hartsop Hall**.

2 The path follows round the back of Hartsop Hall and swings round to the left to join the lane heading towards the campsite at the end of Brothers Water. Cross the little wooden bridge over **Kirkstone Beck** and proceed through the campsite passing the rear entrance to the Brotherswater Inn.

3 Just before the main road at the entrance to the Sykeside camping park take the permitted footpath to **Brothers Water** on the left. The path passes the silted up southern end of Brothers Water before meeting the lakeside once more with the broad shoulder of **Place Fell** to the front and the whale-back ridge of Hartsop above Howe to the left. Enjoy the stroll along the lakeshore path meandering beneath the trees shortly to reach a kissing gate through a fence into a pasture, where the route heads up towards a wall and the road.

(4) Immediately cross the road and on the opposite side follow a finger post signed Public Footpath through a five bar gate. Take

Path through Low Wood

Hartsop Dodd across Brothers Water

the lane between dry stone walls heading towards Hartsop. Initially up a gentle incline only to drop back down again into the village. Pass Bank End cottage and cross a wooden footbridge over **Pasture Beck**,

emerging in the centre of the village onto a metalled road. Turn right up through the village.

(5) Towards the top of the village turn left at a finger post along

Hartsop Hall

a Public Footpath to head up around the back of the village on a surfaced lane passing through a gate, before the lane swings round to the left heading towards **Patterdale**. Above the village there is a stunning view back across to Hartsop Dodd seemingly towering above the village from whence it derived its name and across to Brothers Water. At the "Rathmore" junction, carry straight on the marked footpath and follow the way marked signs around the back of the cottages. Then pass through a gate onto the open fell side following the clear path heading north to catch a glimpse of the upper reaches of Ullswater. Continue through some delightful mixed broad-leafed woodland. Nearing **Angle Tarn Beck** the sound of falling water

Sheep in Low Wood

reaches a climax; climbing the ladder stile the impressive force comes into view. Cross the beck, over the stones if water levels allow or go down the side of the wall for a few yards to cross safely over a wooden bridge at the bottom. Resume the journey along the track towards

Patterdale, resisting the temptation to turn left through a gate.

6 Continue along the stony lane to reach an inverted Y junction. Double back at the junction following the Public Bridleway sign to **Deepdale Bridge**. Cross the bridge over **Goldrill Beck** and turn immediately left to follow the beck side heading back towards Brothers Water. Walk through the fields beside the beck crossing a couple of stiles before emerging over another stile onto the road. Taking care, cross over

Brothers Water, one of the smallest lakes, is relatively shallow with reed and waterlily beds. Originally called Broad Water, the name was changed in the 19th century in memory of two brothers who were drowned in its waters whilst ice skating in 1785, an event that Dorothy Wordsworth recorded in her diary some 20 years later.

Gray Crag across Brothers Waters in winter

Bluebell

the busy road and continue on the other side through a kissing gate, on a permissive path back through the woods to Brothers Water. Enjoy the last half mile of gentle walking on the narrow path through the trees back to the Cow Bridge Car Park.

7 Grisedale from Patterdale

*Enjoy a journey deep into the heart of the fells along
the 'Valley of the pigs'*

The outward journey of this route follows in reverse part of the Coast to Coast Walk – being the section from Grasmere to Patterdale. However this route predates modern walkers as it was an ancient packhorse route between Patterdale and Grasmere via

Grisedale Tarn. It was very familiar to the Wordsworth family and frequently used by them. William's brother John was a ship's master and often spent his leave at Dove Cottage in Grasmere. To return to his ship, John would walk up to the top of Grisedale accompanied by William. Here ,by a large rock,

Level: 🥾
Length: 5 ½ miles (8.6km)
Ascent: 750ft (225m)
Terrain: An easy start on surfaced lane, followed by clear Lakeland paths.
Park and start: Patterdale (GR 394 160)
Refreshments & facilities: Patterdale Hotel.

they would part and John would descend into Patterdale, from there catching a coach to Penrith. John was lost at sea in 1805 in the *Earl of Abergavenny* disaster along with 250 others and William wrote his great 'Elegiac Stanzas', lamenting the death of his brother. In the 1880s the Wordsworth Society arranged for this

Lanty's Tarn

Braestead

Patterdale

A592

Grisedale Beck

Harrison Crag

Birks Crag

Elmhow Crag

1000 m

to be commemorated on the Brothers' Parting Stone with an extract from the poem.

(1) Park either at the George Starkey Hut or the main Car Park opposite the Patterdale Hotel. From here walk back along the road towards St Patrick's Church. Pass the

Patterdale Mountain Rescue Hut

The Coast to Coast Walk is one of the most popular long distance paths in the country. Originally described and defined by Alfred Wainwright the master fell-walker of Pictorial Guide to the Lakes fame, it has amongst the most spectacular scenery of any of Britain's long distance paths.

church on the left and continue along the road with the Old Police House and Patterdale Mountain Rescue Headquarters on the right hand side.

(2) Where the road passes over a beck take the side road up to the left, now keeping the beck to your

right hand side. The road swings around to the right signposted 'Helvellyn and Grisedale Tarn'. This narrow surfaced lane rises quite steeply, with **Grisedale Beck** flowing swiftly in the deep wooden ravine before opening out into **Grisedale** itself.

Grisedale

with a range of outbuildings, pass through a five bar gate and continue along the level heading up the valley. Pass through a series of gates. Grisedale is part of the Dalemain Estate; **St Sunday Crag** now towers to the left, to the right can be seen **Dollywagon Pike**, **Nethermost Pike** and **Striding Edge**. This path along the valley is following the Coast to Coast route which goes from St Bees in the West to Robin Hood's Bay in the East.

(3) Very soon a T-junction is reached, to the right is the path to **Helvellyn** and the return route, but continue straight on the main track up the valley, through a gate signed Private Land – No Parking. A little further on where the track swings to the right leading to a farm, continue on the track up the valley with the wall on the left. At a small farmstead, now holiday cottages,

Upper Grisedale

Falls in Grisedale Beck

remains of mine workings and below, crossing **Grisedale Beck** a wooden bridge. Leave the main track which now continues up to **Grisedale Tarn** and aim for this bridge through what can be wet and boggy ground. Once over the bridge pass through the gate in the wall follow the track up the fellside towards **Eagle Crag**. This is a wide well laid out track which once served the mines, whose spoil heaps can be seen directly ahead on the face of Eagle Crag. At the remains of a building turn right onto a cobbled path which marks the start of our return leg along Grisedale back towards Patterdale. Cross over Nethermost Beck on a wooden footbridge; Place Fell now in the foreground. This is now steady, easy walking undulating through glacial remains.

(4) At the point where Nethermost Beck comes crashing down the fellside on the opposite side of the valley are the

(5) The path passes behind the farm seen on the outbound route, parallel to the intake wall, rising slightly up the fellside and then passing through an ancient cast iron posted gate.

(6) When the path joins the route coming down from **Striding Edge**, take a right turn through a gate in the wall and head down the track which then meets the road leading to the kennels of the Ullswater Hounds. Pass through a kissing gate and onto the tarmaced road. Heading to the right, continue on that road until it meets the main route. Turning left, retrace the route back along the steep lane down towards Patterdale, turning right and the main road for the short walk back to the car.

8 Red Tarn

The walk to Red Tarn from Glenridding provides a fine expedition into the heart of the Eastern fells with breathtaking scenery

Scaling the heights of Helvellyn at over 3000ft is beyond the scope of this book, however for those feeling adventurous and wanting to take in the atmosphere of a true mountain walk, this route to Red Tarn offers a more achievable alternative. Starting from Glenridding and walking up Mires Beck and onto the Birkhouse Moor, the route then leaves the Helvellyn route at the famous Hole-in-the-Wall to visit Red Tarn nestling below Striding Edge and then returning via Greenside Mine. Red Cove is the site where early hill-

Level: 🐾 🐾 🐾
Length: 6 miles (9.5km)
Ascent: 2000 feet (630m)
Terrain: A real mountain climb up to Red Tarn, followed by the descent to Glenridding on good paths.
Park and start: LDNP Car Park in Glenridding (Grid ref 385 170)
Refreshments & facilities: Public houses and tearooms in Glenridding.

walker Charles Gough died in 1805, falling from the head of the cove onto the rocks below. His faithful terrier bitch Foxey stayed with his body until he was discovered three months later. Wordsworth's 'Fidelity' tells the sad tale in full.

Greenside Mine (disused)   Glenridding Dodd
Glenridding
Red Tarn Beck
Glenridding Beck
6
2   1
Birkhouse Moor
Mires Beck
3
Red Tarn
5   4   Hole-in-the-Wall

1000 m

1 Start out from the rear of the Car Park, signed 'Glenridding' past the Glenridding Health Centre. Turn left onto the lane to walk along the road out through the back of the village and past The Travellers Rest, ideally situated for a well deserved drink upon completion of the walk — don't become distracted at this early stage!

2 At the top of the village at the Y junction take the left hand lane signposted to "Helvellyn and Red Tarn". Crossing over the beck, the climbing immediately starts, initially on the surfaced lane next to **Mires Beck**. At the next junction of paths, pass through the gate following the sign "Public Footpath Helvellyn via Mires Beck". Go through the

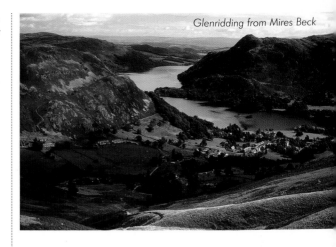

Glenridding from Mires Beck

intake wall using the gate or by climbing over the adjacent stile and take the left hand path to continue the upward journey to **Birkhouse Moor** beside Mires Beck. Even though this is a well-built, pitched

path for the crowds who are heading in the direction of **Striding Edge** and Helvellyn, this is the toughest part of the day having to get straight into climbing before the muscles have had chance to properly warm up.

Perhaps this makes a good excuse to pause half way up to turn and enjoy the retrospective views down to Glenridding and the upper reaches of Ullswater across to **Place Fell** and Arnison Crag and in the distance the Eden Valley and the Pennines.

During the year more than half a million people telephone the Weatherline or look at the website to check on weather conditions for the fell tops of the Lake District National Park. Between December and March, the National Park Authority's fell top assessors trek daily up Helvellyn to record snow, ice and wind conditions above 3000 feet.

Striding Edge and Helvellyn above Red Tarn

(3) Upon cresting the ridge, a wall is reached at a huge cairn marking a T junction of paths - turn right to continue up to Birkhouse Moor. Great views open out over the wall to **St Sunday Crag** and **Fairfield**. The path continues to rise relentlessly next to the wall. The clearly defined main path swings away from the wall which is the better path for walking on. As the path flattens out prepare to have your breath taken away as **Helvellyn** and the pyramidal shape of Catstycam come into view. At this point a faint trod heads off through the grass to the right leading to the marked summit cairn of Birkhouse Moor where 'Wainwright baggers' will

Swirral Barn, Greenside

right leading to the outflow of Red Tarn. This straight path along the flat, gives a pleasant break from the climbing thus far. From this quiet path, watch the crowds heading along Striding Edge like an army of ants silhouetted against the skyline on the ridge. Red Tarn makes a great location to stop for a bit of 'snap', taking time to enjoy the majestic surroundings.

want to make the short 100yard detour to claim the cairn before returning to the main path. The great bowl containing **Red Tarn** with Helvellyn at its peak is laid out, with **Striding Edge** to the left and **Swirral Edge** to the right, leading to the summit of **Catstycam**. The path rejoins the wall, with the

remainder of the route clearly visible; the straight path beneath Striding Edge leading to Red Tarn, and the wide white path back down to Glenridding.

 Just before the famous **'Hole-in-the-Wall'** - now a stile - a clear path veers off to the

 From Red Tarn take the clear path which now returns to Glenridding. Once on the main path below Catstycam, the route makes a long gentle descent on a well made path to **Greenside Mines**- simply follow the clear path downhill all the way! The path swings around the front of Catstycam with Red Tarn Beck bubbling away on the right. As the

Red Tarn

upper mine workings are passed, the path crosses the beck over a wooden footbridge. The route continues along the old mine road with the beck now on the left, where it's worth taking a last look back up the valley to the shapely cone of Catstycam.

6 At Greenside Mine a metal footbridge crosses the beck. Those with fresh legs may wish to keep to the right (southern) bank of the beck back to Glenridding. For those with tired legs, the easier route is to cross the beck and pass through the buildings of Greenside Mine, including **Swirral Barn** and the Youth Hostel, to proceed along the surfaced Mine Road all the way back to Glenridding and that well deserved drink at The Travellers Rest!

Catstycam from the mine road

9 Sheffield Pike

A real mountain walk to the highest point in the book

This his walk visits the highest point of any of the walks in this book, starting with a delightful walk along the shores of the lake before ascending the picturesque Glencoyne valley where the view opens out to the high peaks of Helvellyn and Catstycam. A final pull to the mountain summit at 2232 feet qualifies it in the minds of most people as a true mountain being over 2000 feet. With this amount of ascent a clear day is essential as Sheffield Pike is no place to be in the mist. The return gives an opportunity to explore some of Ullswater's industrial heritage passing by the remains of Greenside Mine before finally strolling down the old mine road back to Glenridding.

Level: 🥾 🥾 🥾
Length: 5 ¾ miles (9km)
Ascent: 2000 feet (600m)
Terrain: After an easy start on the level a long steady pull uphill, followed by a step descent to Greenside Mines and an easy return along a lane.
Park and start: Glenridding LDNP Car Park (GR 385 170).
Refreshments & facilities: Public houses and tearooms in Glenridding.

1 Park in the LDNP Car Park in Glenridding next to the Information Centre. Start by heading back towards the main road towards the lake, turn left to walk along the pavement next to the road. Pass the petrol station and garage as the edge of the village is reached.

2 As the road swings around to the left to leave the village, cross over the road and go down a set of steps to join the lakeshore path

Sheffield Pike from Glencoyne

The native red squirrel is often observed in the woods at the back of Seldom Seen. Its larger grey cousin was introduced to England in the late 1870s from America and is the main cause of decline of the red squirrel by out-competing it for food and transmitting a virus, the squirrel poxvirus, that is lethal to the reds.

which runs through woodland. Keep to the shoreline path as the path rounds **Stybarrow Crag** jutting out into the lake. This gives a lovely viewpoint of Ullswater, especially looking west to Hartsop Dodd and **Arnison Crag** above Patterdale. The path drops and hugs the water's edge for a while

before coming out onto the road. Walk along the road keeping to the right hand side into the face of oncoming traffic. The road crosses over **Mossdale Beck** opposite Hawkhow, at this point leave the road again and take the footpath on the right next to the road.

3 After a couple of hundred yards the path again touches the road. Cross over the road and follow the narrow path signed Public Footpath 'Seldom Seen and Glencoyne'. The path heads up through the bracken and woodland away from the road rising to a gate through a wire fence; pass through and continue on the path up through the woods over the brow of a little outcrop before dropping down to the main track just below.

Ullswater from Stybarrow Crag

height is gained the trees are left behind and at a junction of walls cross over the wooden stile over the one in front and continue on the clear path up the fellside with the wall constantly on the right. Pause to enjoy the retrospective view along Ullswater as you cross over the stile.

(4) Turn left onto the main track heading up to the cottages of **Seldom Seen** above **Glencoyne**. Pass a green painted iron bench dated 1897, commemorating Queen Victoria's Diamond Jubilee which marks a splendid viewpoint across Glencoyne and along Ullswater. As the track swings around to the left away from the lake, you get the first glimpse of

the crags of **Sheffield Pike** high above. The path continues up and around the back of the cottages of Seldom Seen. With a drystone wall on the right, the path rises gently all the way to **Nick Head**, around the back of Sheffield Pike. Prepare for what is a long steady climb of some 1200 feet along the full length of **Glencoyne Valley** beneath Sheffield Pike. As

(5) As the upper reaches of Glencoynedale are reached, level with a hanging valley, pass through a final gate through the

Victoria Jubilee Bench

Upper Glencoynedale

intake wall and the view opens out to the upper reaches of Glencoynedale, with an impressive sheepfold in the valley bottom. Having paused to catch your breath the path continues straight along the fellside gradually rising to **Nick Head**. The path continues its inexorable climb along the side of Sheffield Pike to Nick Head. Eventually reaching the top of the valley the path starts to swing around to the left around the back of Sheffield Pike.

Ullswater from Sheffield Pike

Sheffield Pike summit

6 Nick Head is reached and the view opens out to the pyramidal shape of **Catstycam** with **Helvellyn** behind and the upper Greenside Mine workings. The path forks and to complete the ascent to the summit take the upper left hand of the two paths. This cuts off the corner around Nick Head across some boggy terrain. Reaching the path from Nick Head turn left to follow it uphill to the summit of Sheffield Pike. The path to

the top now through the heather on peat can be wet in places especially after rain. The path steepens bringing the craggy top into view and the summit is reached, with great views along Ullswater, across Place Fell, High Street ridge, then St Sunday Crag and Helvellyn.

7 Having enjoyed the views, retrace your steps back to Nick Head. From here keep straight on one of the indistinct tracks heading towards the footbridge over **Swart Beck** at the mine workings.

8 Arrive at the wooden footbridge over Swart Beck at the base of the spoil heaps of **Greenside Mines**. Cross the beck over the bridge and pick up the old miner's path on

Catstycam from Nick Head

the right hand bank which leads down to Greenside passing by ruined buildings. After a while, as height is lost, the end of Ullswater comes into sight with Glenridding down on the waters edge. The path zig zags downhill rapidly losing height to the Greenside Mine buildings below with evidence of this former industrialised landscape all

around. By the disused water sluices meet the main path.

9 Reaching the old mine road, turn left and, gently descend to the village with Glenridding Beck below to the right. Weary souls may be tempted by The Travellers Rest at the top of the village.

10 Aira Force & Gowbarrow

A popular destination for visitors with an extended walk giving outstanding views along Ullswater

Aira Force and Gowbarrow Fell wholly belong to Ullswater. This knobbly little fell stands proud on the banks of Ullswater. This short but popular walk amply justifies the effort in climbing to the summit with outstanding views along Ullswater and across its hinterland to Dockray and Matterdale.

Level: 🥾 🥾
Length: 4 ¼ miles (6.75km)
Ascent: 1400 feet in total (430m)
Terrain: Surfaced paths around Aira Force and clear mountain paths across Gowbarrow.
Park and start: Aira Force N T Car Park (Grid ref 401201).
Refreshments & facilities: Aira Force Tearooms, Public Toilets in Car Park.

Bridge over Aira Force

1 Leave through the back of the car park, past the National Trust information point; proceed through a wrought iron gate onto the National Trust Aira Force Estate. At the clearing take the path crossing the bridge over **Aira Beck** and proceed up the right hand bank to **Aira**

Ullswater from Gowbarrow Fell in winter

Aira Force

Force. The walk now follows the well laid tourist path alongside the beck through mixed broadleaf woodland. On approaching the falls you are met with a crescendo of sound from the crashing water. The lower bridge was erected in 1931 by the family and friends of Cecil Spring-Rice, Ambassador to the USA during World War I. Take your time to enjoy the falls and then take the often slippery steps leading steeply out of the gorge. At the top of the steps turn right to reach the upper bridge.

In the 1780's the Howard family of Greystoke Castle renovated an old Pele Tower close to the Ullswater shore into what is now Lyulph's Tower. During the 19th century they created an arboretum below the force, planting specimen conifers from all over the world, including a Sitka Spruce, now 118 feet high.

(2) From the upper bridge take the middle path heading towards **Gowbarrow**. Follow the path at the edge of the trees and just before a bench, a path joins from the left. Take this, doubling back to head towards a gate in 30 yards, cross the adjacent style, onto the fellside, and

after a further 20 yards a crossroad of paths is reached. Take the right path heading up the fellside through the bracken. The clear path continues steadily gaining height to reach the summit of **Green Hill** with ever widening views along Ullswater. After admiring this spectacular view continue up the green gently rising path. At a

minor junction, keep on the main broader path swinging upwards to the left. From the unmistakable summit cairn of Green Hill the Ordnance Survey point on the summit of Gowbarrow can be seen. Take the faint narrow path over open moorland to reach the true summit of Gowbarrow marked with a National

Lyulph's Tower

Aira Force & Gowbarrow

Mist over Ullswater from Yew Crag

Ullswater from Gowbarrow Fell

Trust Plaque OS No. BM1790. On a clear day there will be extensive views along Ullswater to Pooley Bridge and beyond the Eden Valley and the Pennines.

3 From the summit take the clear path heading east down towards Ullswater, initially heading towards a wall. Keep on this path running parallel with the wall gradually losing height all the while. As **Hallin Fell** comes into full view on the opposite side of Ullswater continue starting to swing around to the right along the face of Gowbarrow. The path crosses a narrow wooden footbridge over a steep and narrow gulley down the fellside and meanders around the front of the fell. Pass a cairn marking a magnificent viewpoint.

Lyulph's Tower comes into view down below and the path starts to lose height in line with the tower, to head down back towards the Aira Force estate.

4 Upon reaching the boundary of the Aira Force estate simply cross the stile over the fence to rejoin the outward tourist path, and reverse the outward journey on the gravel path back to the car.

Sheep on Gowbarrow Fell

Sheep on Gowbarrow Fell in winter